MAYOR

By Jacqueline Laks Gorman
Reading consultant: Susan Nations, M.Ed.,
author/literacy coach/consultant in literacy development

WEEKLY READER®
PUBLISHING

Please visit our web site at www.garethstevens.com
For a free color catalog describing our list of high-quality books,
call 1-800-542-2595 (USA) or 1-800-387-3178 (Canada). Our fax: 1-877-542-2596

Library of Congress Cataloging-in-Publication Data
Laks Gorman, Jacqueline.
   Mayor / by Jacqueline Laks Gorman.
      p. cm. — (Know your government)
   Includes bibliographical references and index.
   ISBN-10: 1-4339-0093-9   ISBN-13: 978-1-4339-0093-8 (lib. bdg.)
   ISBN-10: 1-4339-0121-8   ISBN-13: 978-1-4339-0121-8 (soft cover)
   1. Mayors—United States—Juvenile literature. I. Title.
JS356.G67   2008
352.23'2160973—dc22   2008045566

This edition first published in 2009 by
Weekly Reader® Books
An Imprint of Gareth Stevens Publishing
1 Reader's Digest Road
Pleasantville, NY 10570-7000 USA

Copyright © 2009 by Gareth Stevens, Inc.

Executive Managing Editor: Lisa M. Herrington
Editors: Brian Fitzgerald and Barbara Kiely Miller
Creative Director: Lisa Donovan
Senior Designer: Keith Plechaty
Photo Researcher: Kim Babbitt
Publisher: Keith Garton

Photo credits: cover & title page Ben Rose/WireImage; p. 5 Joseph Connoly/Getty Images; p. 6 Ramin Talaie/
Corbis; p. 7 Courtesy of the Gracie Mansion Museum; p. 9 Ray Abrams-Pool/Getty Images; p. 10 Dana
White/Photo Edit; p. 11 Gregg Andersen; p.12 Jupiter Images; p. 13 David McNew/Getty Images; p. 15 Tasos
Katopodis/Getty Images; p. 16 Courtesy mayor's office, Muskogee, Oklahoma; p. 17 Erik S. Lesser/Getty
Images; p. 19 Library of Congress; p. 20 Bettmann/Corbis; p. 21 Spencer Platt/Getty Images.

Printed in the United States of America

1 2 3 4 5 6 7 8 9 10 09 08

Cover Photo: Shirley Jackson was elected mayor of Atlanta, Georgia, in 2002. She was the city's first female
African American mayor.

TABLE OF CONTENTS

Chapter 1: Who Are Mayors? 4

Chapter 2: What Does a Mayor Do? 8

Chapter 3: How Does a Person Become a Mayor? 14

Chapter 4: Famous Mayors 18

Glossary 22

To Find Out More 23

Index 24

Words that appear in the glossary are printed in **boldface** type the first time they appear in the text.

CHAPTER 1

Who Are Mayors?

The United States has thousands of towns and cities. Each town or city has its own government. Many towns and cities have a **mayor**. The mayor is the head of a town or city government.

From 1996 to 2002, Sarah Palin was the mayor of Wasilla, Alaska. In 2008, she ran for vice president of the United States.

The mayor meets with other mayors from around the state. The mayor meets with people in other parts of the country, too. The mayor has power only in his or her town or city, however.

Towns and cities can have different kinds of governments. Some mayors have more powers than others. Some towns and cities do not have mayors at all. Groups of people run the government in those places.

Mayors sometimes meet with foreign leaders. In 2008, New York City mayor Michael Bloomberg (right) met with Gordon Brown. Brown is the leader of the United Kingdom.

Gracie Mansion is the official home of the mayor of New York City.

A mayor lives and works in his or her town or city. In some cities, the mayor works in a building called City Hall. Some cities provide houses for their mayors. Other mayors live in their own homes.

CHAPTER 2

What Does a Mayor Do?

Town and city governments do many jobs. They may control the police and fire departments. They may run the schools and libraries. Some cities and towns provide clean water and collect garbage. Mayors make sure that those services run smoothly.

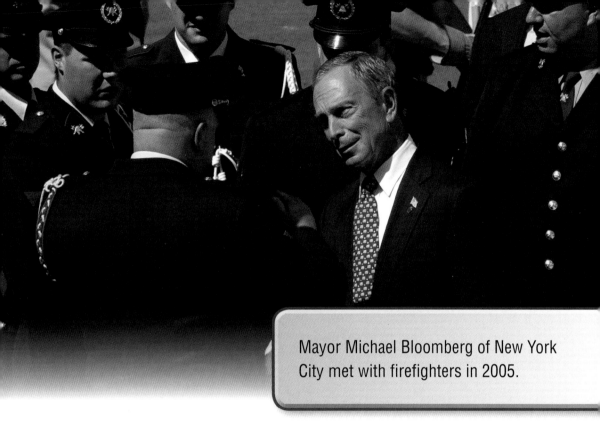

Mayor Michael Bloomberg of New York City met with firefighters in 2005.

Many towns and cities have a **council**. The people of the town or city **elect**, or choose, the people on the council. The mayor works with the council to run the town or city. The mayor may lead the meetings of the council.

City council members often hold meetings. They listen to people talk about issues in the community.

The council passes new laws for the city or town. In some places, mayors must sign the laws to make them official. In other places, mayors do not have that power. Sometimes, people in cities and towns vote on ideas for new laws.

Police officers help enforce the law in cities and towns.

A mayor makes sure that people follow the law. Mayors work with the police department and the **courts**. The courts decide whether people broke the law.

Town and city budgets include money for parks and playgrounds.

Town and city governments spend a lot of money every year. The mayor may prepare the **budget**. The budget is a plan for spending the money. The council votes to pass the budget. The budget includes money for schools, parks, and other important areas.

Mayors oversee the work of many people. Mayors may choose the heads of town or city departments. Mayors also take charge during emergencies in their cities.

In 2008, wildfires hit Los Angeles, California. Mayor Antonio Villaraigosa visited areas where the fires had destroyed homes.

CHAPTER 3

How Does a Person Become a Mayor?

Cities and towns have different ways of choosing a mayor. In most places, voters elect the mayor. In others, the council may pick one of its members to be the mayor.

Richard M. Daley (left) has been the mayor of Chicago, Illinois, for many years. In 2006, he was elected to a sixth term.

Different mayors may serve for different lengths of time. The **term** for some mayors is two years. The term for others is four or six years. In some places, mayors can serve only two terms. In other places, mayors can serve as many terms as they want.

Candidates are people who run for office. Candidates for mayor travel around their city or town. They give speeches and share their ideas. Candidates may have **debates** about issues in the city or town.

In 2008, John Tyler Hammons was elected mayor of Muskogee, Oklahoma. He was only 19 years old!

In 2002, Shirley Franklin (left) was sworn in as mayor of Atlanta, Georgia.

Candidates in a big city may run ads on TV. In small towns, they may go to voters' homes to talk to them. On Election Day, people in the town or city vote. The candidate who gets the most votes is elected mayor.

CHAPTER 4

Famous Mayors

Many mayors did great things for their cities. They became well known to the whole country. Some mayors became **governor** of their state. Others held other important jobs in government.

Some mayors were later elected president of the United States. In 1882, Grover Cleveland became mayor of Buffalo, New York. Two years later, he was elected U.S. president.

Calvin Coolidge was mayor of Northampton, Massachusetts, from 1910 to 1911. He later became the 30th U.S. president.

Grover Cleveland was elected U.S. president in 1884 and 1892.

Tom Bradley was mayor of Los Angeles, California. He helped unite people of many races and backgrounds.

Tom Bradley was elected mayor of Los Angeles, California, in 1973. He was the first African American mayor of the city. He was mayor for 20 years. That is longer than anyone else.

Mayor Rudolph Giuliani helped people stay strong during a tough time.

Rudolph Giuliani was mayor of New York City on September 11, 2001. On that day, many people lost their lives in attacks on buildings in the city. Mayor Giuliani was a strong leader for his city. People across the country and the world admired him.

Glossary

budget: a plan for how to spend and make money

candidates: people who are running for office

council: a group of people who are elected to make decisions for a city or town

courts: the places where legal cases are heard and decided

debates: formal arguments between candidates about important issues facing the country

elect: to choose leaders by voting

governor: the head of a state government

mayor: the head of a town or city government

term: a set period of time that a person serves in office

To Find Out More

Books

The City Mayor. Our Government (series). Terri Degezelle
(Capstone Press, 2005)

What's a Mayor? First Guide to Government (series). Nancy Harris
(Heinemann, 2007)

Rudolph Giuliani. Rookie Biographies (series). Wil Mara
(Children's Press, 2003)

Web Site

The Democracy Project
www.pbskids.org/democracy/mygovt/index.html
Find out how the government affects you, including your
city government.

Publisher's note to educators and parents: Our editors have carefully reviewed these web sites to ensure that they are suitable for children. Many web sites change frequently, however, and we cannot guarantee that a site's future contents will continue to meet our high standards of quality and educational value. Be advised that children should be closely supervised whenever they access the Internet.

Index

Bloomberg, Michael 6, 9
Bradley, Tom 20
Brown, Gordon 6
budgets 12
Cleveland, Grover 19
Coolidge, Calvin 19
council 9, 10, 12
courts 11
Daley, Richard M. 15

Franklin, Shirley 17
Giuliani, Rudolph 21
Gracie Mansion 7
Hammons, John Tyler 16
laws 10, 11
Palin, Sarah 5
Villaraigosa, Antonio 13

About the Author

Jacqueline Laks Gorman is a writer and an editor. She grew up in New York City. She has worked on many kinds of books and has written several children's series. She lives with her husband, David, and children, Colin and Caitlin, in DeKalb, Illinois. She registered to vote when she turned 18 and votes in every election.